Move *into the* Magic

✳

A Guide to Discovering Your Life's Mission

MAXINE TAYLOR

ISBN 978-1-4276-5156-3

Cover Design by envisionarydesigns.com
Interior Design by bigAdesigns.com
Photos by Rob Melvin

To Rob
I couldn't have done it without you.

Acknowledgements

"Thank you" doesn't even begin to tell it: To Rob, Deb, Vic and Betsy, my "advisory board"... Thank you for your years of loving support, brilliant insights, and loyal friendship.

To Peggi, Loren, Marilyn and Hope... Thank you for sharing your stories with me and allowing me to include your personal journeys in this book.

Move *into the* Magic

CONTENTS

Why Is This Book for You?

I f you are reading this powerful book, it is because you are ready for more than a change; you are ready for a quantum leap forward. You may think you are ready for a new job, a move to a new location or even a new romance— and maybe you are. But, if you are reading this book, you are ready to be *transformed*, and this book is designed to help you do just that.

Maybe you have been reading self help books and searching for answers for years. Many of these books are quite good.

I have read them myself. Each one gave me a piece of the puzzle.

What makes this book unique is that it gives you the whole picture. It shows you the cause of the problem and gives you the solution. It takes you from birth to the present and shows you, step by step, how to identify and let go of the commitments that have run your life and created your life's story. In addition, it gives you a technique to rewrite your life the way you want it to be. This is empowering.

Once you have let go of your story, you are ready for what you have been looking for: why you came here to planet Earth. Many people sense they have a mission, something larger than what they can verbalize or define. They do. So do you. Your mission is your destiny. This book will help you discover it.

If you are reading this book, you are ready to change your entire outlook, your entire life. You are ready to know who you really are, how unique and wonderful you are, what your mission is, what has been holding you back and how to end it.

Most of all, if you are reading this book, you are ready to move into the Magic—the Magic that is you. Welcome to your own personal adventure!

My Journey

I tell people that when I moved from Miami to Atlanta in 1966, my life changed. Actually, it was much more profound than that—my life *began*.

1966 was the year I "stepped on the path" and began my search for Truth. So much of what I was taught to believe as a child changed. My eyes opened to a deeper, more synchronistic pattern of life, and my desire to understand this synchronicity was born.

I wanted to know who we are and why we are here. I did not realize it at the time, but this is when I became a student of human and spiritual nature.

Within two years of my move to Atlanta, I was part of a spiritual group led by an Episcopal priest. We studied metaphysics, and developed our own psychic talents and abilities. This group became the original members of the Atlanta Institute of Metaphysics.

Once I began studying astrology, it quickly became clear to me that I *had* to leave my career as a high school French and Spanish teacher, and become a professional astrologer. However, back in the 1960s, astrology was considered fortune-telling all over the country, and a fortune-telling license was not only exorbitant, but insulting. So I had the law changed in Atlanta, and became Georgia's first licensed astrologer. In 1970, I left public school teaching to devote full time to my private astrology practice. However, I continued to teach—astrology.

I became part of a spiritual school where I learned how to identify and release my childhood programming. This school showed me both heaven and hell, and gave me invaluable insight into people.

I discovered how to read my clients' hidden parental messages in their birth charts. This opened up a new dimension of chart interpretation, which became my specialty. I wrote a book about this for astrologers. In fact, I wrote five astrology books which were published by the American Federation of Astrologers. I became passionate about helping people see and transform their lives, and gave workshops on this. I took these life-transforming workshops out of the realm of astrology, and presented them to the public.

I became CNN's on-air astrologer and gave live political forecasts.

I was ordained as a minister. This allowed me to conduct loving spiritual ceremonies, from marriages and commitment ceremonies to funerals.

One of my greatest passions is energy healing. The miracle that takes place when two people are vibrating at the same frequency and have the same intent is true magic.

I studied different types of energy healing with talented teachers. Then, I created Star Matrix, my own healing method.

I now understand why I moved to Atlanta in 1966. Today, I am Georgia's first licensed astrologer, a spiritual coach, an energy healer, an ordained minister, a public speaker and an author. I use these vehicles to assist people to see their story, release it, rewrite it, and to discover their mission and move into the Magic. This is why I came here.

Maxine

The Road Map

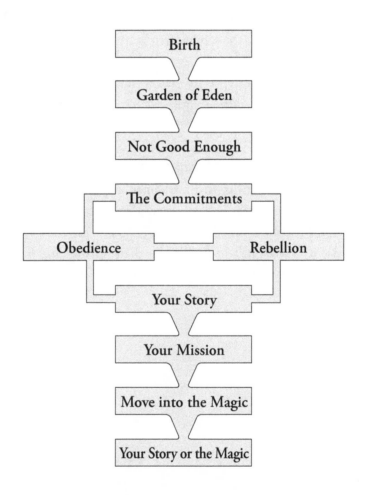

Birth

Garden of Eden

Not Good Enough

The Commitments

Obedience   Rebellion

Your Story

Your Mission

Move into the Magic

Your Story or the Magic

Introduction

You are infinite, immortal Spirit in an earthbound body. This is the truth. Everything else is a lie. When you get this on the cellular level, your life changes.

You came here to planet Earth with a mission—a mission hidden from your conscious mind, buried beneath the story you chose prior to birth and live every day.

This story repeats itself over and over again—different people, different settings, same story. For most people, their story begins at birth and ends at death. But some people know they can change their story. This book will show you how to do just that.

At some point you may have an ah-ha! moment in which you recognize the repetitious, predictable pattern of your life. You may even see where this began in your childhood. This revelation will be life-changing. From this moment on, you will see everyone and everything differently.

You will observe the people around you—your family, friends, co-workers, neighbors—with new eyes. You will hear them reciting their story. It is predictable and repetitious, and might go something like this, "Nobody loves me", "They give me the responsibility, but not the authority", "I'm right and everyone else is wrong", "I was molested as a child", "I get it and lose it", "They loved my brother more than me", etc. As you watch and listen to people, their story is like a movie. Each time you see them, they pop the DVD into the player and the story repeats itself. You can almost give their movie a name and a theme song. You can script it because their story never changes. It began in childhood and has repeated itself (same parts, different actors) ever since.

Some people recognize their never-ending, constantly-repeating story, but do not want to change it. They do not want to solve their problems; they just want to live comfortably within them. Some people recognize their pattern but do not know they have the power to change it. However, most people do not recognize the repetitious pattern of their lives.

For some, though, there comes a time when they simply cannot take it any more. Even if they do not recognize the repetitive nature of their story, they know they cannot tolerate it one more day. While their symptoms may vary, they experience one or all of the following. They:

- are bored with their life and the people in it
- are frustrated
- are angry
- flip between anger and depression
- feel hopeless and lack a reason to go on
- are ready for a new start, a new adventure, whether it is a career, a new love, etc.
- are sick and/or their body hurts
- are on "hold" and do not want to do a thing

Are you one of these people? If so, you are ready to see your story clearly and end it. You are ready to consciously rewrite it and live your life *your* way.

This book will guide you, step by step, through an incredibly simple process that has transformed the lives of countless people.

This process:

- gets right to the source of the problem
- works fast
- helps you see your story
- frees you to recognize and stop listening to your critical, fearful left brain
- helps you move into the Magic and stay there
- gives you a simple technique to keep you on track

So now you are ready to begin.

PART 1

✸

Be My Buddy

✷

While you can absolutely do every step in this powerful book by yourself, a great way to do them is with a trusted, supportive friend: a buddy. When you speak, your buddy will be able to hear things you may not realize you have said, key things that can break you loose and trigger an ah-ha! moment. And you can do the same for him or her.

If you have known your buddy awhile, he or she can fill in the blanks you may have overlooked and give you the missing piece of the puzzle. Your buddy can ask you questions you have never asked yourself, questions that open your eyes and give you a new perspective. In turn, you can do the same.

Whether you move through this book by yourself or with a buddy, your body language will indicate when you are approaching that moment when your answer is ready to surface. You will either speak more slowly or you will trip over your words; your eyes will glaze over or close; you will lean forward in your seat and become more animated or you will sit back and your words will come slowly until suddenly, you get your answer and everything stops for a few seconds. This is palpable, visible and powerful. And it is thrilling to both experience and observe.

By yourself or with a buddy, have a wonderful, exciting adventure as you move into the Magic.

In the Beginning...

✴

While there are always exceptions to every rule, what I am about to share with you is true for most people. When you were born, the most important person in your life was your mother. She was your all. She provided food, love, security, warmth and all good things. She loved you and, as a result, you loved yourself and were happy. You were an inseparable team. Where she went, you went. Your days consisted of doing what children do: you played. Life was idyllic. It was the proverbial Garden of Eden.

Then one day, between the ages of three and six, while you were playing, you became curious and stepped out on your own without her. You did not do anything wrong, you simply moved forward to explore and expand your world. However, you acted independently (without your mother), and she lost control over you. This upset her enormously. She may have cried, gotten angry, or turned her back on you. At that moment, her reaction told you that you had done something wrong and that you were, therefore, bad (for upsetting her by acting independently).

The shock and pain of having inadvertently hurt your mother was traumatic and hypnotic. It was, in fact, a turning point in your life. Some people call this your original wounding. You were figuratively thrown out of the Garden of Eden, and your life was no longer the same.

You never meant to hurt your mother. You were just playing. However, it was too late. From that moment on you accepted that you were bad. You had to get good enough to recapture her love and return to the Garden of Eden. How did you do this? By curbing your natural curiosity, independence and free spirit, and doing what she wanted. You did this by silently, possibly subconsciously, making the commitment to obey her and allow her to control you. While everyone's commitment to their mother is different, they all involve some form of holding themselves back in order to get good enough.

This was your first commitment, and set the stage for subsequent commitments. It is in your cells and, unless you have already identified it and let it go, it is still running your life.

You made this commitment to your mother to prove you were good enough to be forgiven. You felt that if she would just forgive you, you could forgive yourself, return to the Garden of Eden, and life would be as it was before. If she would just love you the way she did when you were young, you could love yourself. If she would just give you permission to explore, to soar, to be yourself, you would be free to do so. Without her permission, you are locked into trying to get good enough, even if she is no longer living. Without her forgiveness, you are controlled by your commitment to her because, in the back of your mind, you are bad (for having upset her). Without her forgiveness, you atone and punish yourself.

Some children, after trying, recognize that they will never be able to do enough to get good enough. Rather than continue to try to prove that they *are* and give their mother what she wants, they rebel. Their unspoken statement is, "You think I'm bad? Ha! Just watch! I'll show you bad!" Even though they are rebelling against the Bad Message, it is still alive and well, and their commitment to their mother is still running them. This rebellion continues as they grow up and becomes a pattern in their lives.

Some people flip between submission to and rebellion against the Bad Message. Either way, it is still controlling them.

Your commitment to your mother sets the pattern for all subsequent commitments, and leads to the different roles you may have chosen to play in order to get good enough, such as surrogate mother, martyr, victim, hero, superstar, high achiever, failure, pleaser, avenger, authority, hypochondriac, etc.

The Bad Message marks the end of your idyllic childhood and the beginning of the never-ending, constantly-repeating story of your life.

The Bad Message

*

The trauma of your original Bad Message is locked in your cells. Every time you make a mistake, particularly if you do not know you have done so, the story of your life replays and returns to the cell memory of the Bad Message you got from your mother. Feelings of confusion, abandonment, guilt, fear, hopelessness, etc., resurface and hold you in check. In a flash, you return, mentally and emotionally, to that moment in time when you believed you were bad. If you were three years old when you got this message, you think and react as a three year old. Some people live their lives at this age. Just look around you and you will see them: adults in their 40s, 50s and 60s thinking and reacting like children.

Usually, you re-experience the Bad Message when you begin a new venture: start a new job, improve your appearance, get married, etc. The fear of stepping out and acting independently is so strong that you can actually sabotage your success by reliving the Bad Message and symbolically repeating the scenario that has run your life.

Even if you have rebelled against it, you have accepted the Bad Message. Every time you try to move forward, act independently, follow your dream—or even dare to dream— the subconscious memory of being bad for having hurt your mother kicks in and you are back in childhood. You can punish yourself by getting sick, hurting yourself, starting an argument with a friend or loved one, etc. Just the thought of moving forward can fill you with such fear that you do not even want to attempt it. Even if she is no longer living, the Bad Message remains in place until you are consciously aware of it and let it go.

The Bad Message is the cause of the belief that you are not good enough. The belief that you are not good enough keeps you questioning yourself, asking "Who do I think I am? What makes me think I'm capable of _____ or even deserve to attempt it?"

This scene replays over and over again, and it can be triggered by anyone who subconsciously reminds you of your mother: a boss, a friend, even a stranger. It will continue to repeat itself until you recognize that it is just the same old story.

8

The people, locations and situations may be different, but the message is the same: If you act independently and leave your mother, you will upset her, and this will make you bad. You will then have to atone by taking care of her and staying with her, either physically, emotionally, and/or mentally.

* *Peggi*

Peggi, a wise and knowledgeable woman, has not only been a student of truth since she was a little girl, but has had the courage to take a stand for it.

Peggi was raised in a family that was steeped in a very strict, fundamentalist religion which taught that a disobedient child was a bad child. She was to obey God's will by obeying her mother, and if she was not doing God's will, she was doing Satan's. The penalty was ostracism from her church, her friends and her family. Since her religion decreed that church members were only supposed to be friends with other church members, ostracism meant being totally alone in the community. It was this fear of being ostracized that kept Peggi and her entire religious community in line.

Peggi's Bad Message began when she was only six months old. She pulled herself up to a standing position at the stove, reached up, and was severely burned by hot water. From this incident, she learned that it was dangerous for her to reach out and step forward.

Her Bad Message culminated when she was around three years old. She disobeyed her mother by refusing to put on her nightgown. Her mother became angry and severely beat her. This incident taught Peggi that if she did not do what her mother wanted, she would be physically hurt.

From both incidents, she learned that it was her own fault for being burned and beaten because she acted independently.

The religion in which Peggi was raised teaches that only a limited number of people will be good enough to ascend to heaven, so in order to get good enough, she became a pleaser and took on that role. She learned to act differently, depending on who she was with. By pleasing others, she believed she would be safe, she would be good enough, and she would go to heaven. Another role she took on which goes hand-in-hand with the pleaser role is that of caretaker. She realized that she would have to take care of not only herself, but everyone in her family. And she did.

*Loren

Loren is a delightful, funny woman with a zest for life. She is a natural intuitive, healer and nurturer. When she first became my student, she was forty-four, she had moved back in with her parents for financial reasons, and was working in a deli.

While Loren does not remember this story, it was told to her so often during her childhood that she recalls it viscerally.

When she was a child, her family lived in New York City, in an apartment building on Central Park, right next door to the hotel where President John F. Kennedy stayed when he was in town. Loren was an outgoing, enthusiastic child who had made friends with the doorman of her apartment building.

One day, when she, her mother and her baby brother were returning from their walk, Loren ran into what she thought was her apartment building, yelling for her friend, the doorman. However, instead of running into her building, she ran into the hotel next door. JFK was evidently in residence because there were secret service men all over the lobby. As she raced in, calling the doorman's name, followed by her mother who was wheeling her baby brother in his stroller, the secret service men pulled out their guns. While her mother froze in horror, Loren was unfazed. Once the secret service men realized that the commotion was caused by a child, they put away their guns and she got a lollipop.

As she told this story, it was clear that she had been reprimanded by her mother. From this incident, Loren got the message that her enthusiasm, her joy, and her being the center of attention were a problem for her mother. From then on, Loren held herself back, curbed her natural self-expression, and believed that it was wrong to go for what she wanted. This set the stage for her to take on the role of surrogate mother to the world.

*Marilyn

Marilyn is happily married and has a teenage daughter with whom she and her husband have a wonderful relationship. She is a dynamic, hard-working, responsible, successful business woman. She is also a very funny person who would do anything to help her friends.

When I mentioned her Bad Message, she knew exactly what it was. There were two incidents involved, one positive; the other negative.

The positive incident set the stage for the negative one. It occurred when she was three years old and her younger sister was one year old. Her mother had to run across the street to a neighbor's house to borrow an egg, so she put Marilyn in charge. She spoke to her as if she were an adult and told her she knew that she (Marilyn) would follow her instructions to the letter. She told Marilyn to stand at the screen door and hold her younger sister's hand till she returned, which was probably just a few minutes later. Marilyn loved being treated as an adult, and did exactly as she was told. Ever since then, she has acted like a responsible adult, taking care of others.

The actual Bad Message, the negative part of this story, occurred shortly after the positive incident. Walter the painter was at their house, painting the walls. Marilyn went up to him and asked, "What's a vagina?" (Marilyn confessed to me that she already knew what a vagina was. She just wanted to shock him.) Her mother was appalled that Marilyn would ask something so outrageous. She raised her voice, gave Marilyn the "evil eye", and ignored her.

To this day, Marilyn still shocks people with her outrageous sense of humor, but underneath, feels there is something wrong with her. The irony is that her mother says outrageous things, too!

*Hope

Hope is a gentle, loving, divorced mother of two wonderful young children. She is a natural caregiver, and has her degree in nursing. When she became my student, she had been maligned and mistreated at work, and forced to leave her job as Care Coordinator through no fault of her own. She had also ended her relationship with her boyfriend. She was ready for a new start.

When she was three years old, she became so ill that she almost died. From what she was later told, this is the incident that gave her her Bad Message. She was not allowed to leave (through death), but was to stay here, protect her mother and take care of her family. This incident reinforced her belief that she was born to take care of her mother, and told her that she was not allowed to do things her way.

Releasing the Bad Message

Although I have explained the simple releasing and acceptance techniques in the next two chapters, let's apply them here with the Bad Message.

Just move into that place within yourself where you feel safe, protected and secure, such as your heart or your stomach. Ask your mind to show you the first time you accepted that you were bad. If you cannot immediately remember the very first time, start with any childhood incident and keep working backwards until you come to the first one. If that eludes you, simply go with the earliest one you remember. After all, this scene has repeated itself hundreds of times in your life.

This event has been locked in your cells and, at this point in your journey, it is ready to leave. All you have to do is allow it to do so. This will be easy because your Bad Message is simply a lie you accepted when you were very young and very vulnerable. It is not who you are. Remember: the truth is that you are infinite, immortal spirit in an earthbound body. How can spirit possibly be bad? It is not possible.

When you have identified the event in which you received your Bad Message, you are going to release it to (your concept of) God. Allow yourself to get in touch with the event and feel it for just a few seconds. Then say, either silently or out loud, "God (or "Universal Spirit", "Source Energy", "Jesus", "Heavenly Father", whatever words describe God to you), I totally release my Bad Message to you." Then relax your entire body and feel the energy from this event naturally move up from your stomach, chest, throat or wherever it has been stored, until it reaches the top of your head. Relax the top of your head and let it go. It will do this all by itself; simply let it leave. This will take only a minute or so to do.

When it is gone from your cells, you will feel lighter, freer, and happier. You may feel tingly; you will certainly feel better.

Accepting the Good Message

Now it is time to replace the Bad Message with the truth. So, once again, drop down to that place within yourself where you feel safe, protected and secure. The acceptance technique is simple and gentle. Just relax your body and, as you say the following acceptance (or one of your choice), either verbally or nonverbally, let the energy from the words you have spoken pour down through your body, from the top of your head into every cell of your body and out through the soles of your feet:

"I totally accept that I am infinite, immortal Spirit in an

earthly body. I am good, I have always been good and I will always be good."

After doing these two simple steps, people are changed. Their faces glow, they are radiant and happy, and they even look younger!

The Releasing Technique

✦

The releasing technique is incredibly simple. Do not let its simplicity fool you. This technique is so powerful that it can change your life in one minute. I have been teaching it for over thirty years, and its transformative power operates every time.

The beauty of this technique is threefold:

1) You *do it yourself.* You do not need anyone's help, and

2) You can do it anywhere, any time, and

3) It takes only a minute or so.

When you are ready to let go of a commitment or a belief that is destructive to you, you know it because you feel it as a pressure in your body. The longer you wait to release it, the stronger and more powerful the pressure becomes until it can actually be painful. You might feel it as a headache, a knot in your stomach, a weight on your chest, a pain in your back, an overall tenseness, etc. This is your body telling you that the commitment or belief is ready to leave.

You release this commitment or belief to (your concept of) God so that you can be free of it. Because everyone's concept of God is different, you choose the words that feel best to you. The words I use are simply suggestions. Your own words are the ones that count.

The actual technique is simple and gentle; you do not have to do a thing but allow the commitment or belief to leave. It will do this naturally. All you do is create the space for this to happen.

Start by putting your attention on that place within yourself where you feel safe, protected and secure, such as your heart or your stomach. Then identify what you want to let go of. Releasing takes place on an emotional level, so when you have identified what you want to release, simply allow yourself to feel it. You are not going to wallow in it; you are just going to experience it for a few seconds in order to connect with it.

Once you feel it, say, either silently or out loud, "God (or "Universal Spirit", "Source Energy", "Jesus", "Heavenly Father", whatever words you use to describe God), I totally release _____ to you." Or you can also simply release it to the universe. Then relax your entire body and feel the energy naturally move up from your stomach, chest, throat or wherever it has been stored. When it reaches the top of your head, relax your head and let it move up and out. It does this all by itself; all you have to do is allow it leave. This entire process takes only a minute or so.

Once the commitment or belief is released, you know it because your symptoms are gone: if you were tense, you are now relaxed; if you were crying, you are now smiling or even laughing; if you were angry, you are now happy. You may feel tingly; you certainly feel better. Sometimes it can take a few minutes for all of your original symptoms to leave. This is not unusual, so be patient and give yourself the time you need.

> Maddy's father was her hero. She turned to him for advice and made him the most important man in her life. Her commitment to him was to **make him her authority and not surpass him in her career.** However, her father was a salesman and Maddy was a highly successful entrepreneur. When Maddy saw that she had failed to live up to her commitment to her father and had clearly surpassed him in her career, she became depressed and cried.
>
> However, the moment she released her commitment to her father, her burden was lifted. Her depression left and she stopped crying. She no longer felt guilty for being a success, and was able to recognize how proud her father was of her.

The Acceptance Technique

✴

The acceptance technique is also incredibly simple. Again, do not let its simplicity fool you. The power of the acceptance technique cannot be overstated.

After you have released the negative, it is time to replace it with its opposite, the positive. The acceptance completes the process.

Once again, put your attention on that place within yourself where you feel safe, protected and secure, such as your heart or your stomach. Identify the words you are going to accept and feel how good they feel. Say, either silently or out loud, "God (or "Universal Spirit", "Source Energy", "Jesus", "Heavenly Father", whatever words you use to describe God), I totally accept _____." Or you can say these words to the universe. Then, relax your body and let the energy from the words you have just spoken pour down from the top of your head into every cell of your body and out the soles of your feet.

People often say the acceptance feels wonderful. This is an understatement. By filling up your cells with positive energy you replenish the void created by releasing the negative. You feel balanced, happy and complete.

These two simple, yet powerful, steps feel wonderful because they are so freeing. The best part is that you can use them whenever and wherever something or someone upsets you. They are designed to immediately diffuse the situation and turn it around.

After doing the releasing and acceptance techniques, you will be noticeably changed. You will feel calmer, happier and more peaceful. Your face will glow, you will be radiant, and you will even look younger!

The power of the acceptance technique is that it can stand alone. It does not have to be combined with the releasing technique.

For example, let's say you have done a releasing and acceptance about an upsetting situation, but you are still aggravated because the person involved has not changed. The acceptance technique can turn the situation around in an instant.

If someone yells at you and will not apologize, or if they act condescendingly and refuse to treat you with respect, just accept them as they are. That's it. After all, that is how they are. You are upset because you are resisting how they are and want them to change. When you accept them as they are, you are not condoning their actions; you are not saying they are right and you are wrong. You are acknowledging that they are the way they are. Period. The acceptance frees you from resisting and trying to change them. Most of all, it restores your happiness.

> Sally and Steve dated for several years. Sally wanted very much to marry Steve, but Steve, having been badly hurt by his ex-wife, did not want to get married again. Ever. In addition, even though Sally wanted to marry him, there were some things about Steve she did not like and wanted him to change. Steve, in turn, was critical of her. The more she criticized him and pushed for marriage, the more he pulled back and returned her criticism. Finally, they became so angry at one another they broke up.
>
> That week, Sally worked with me and I shared the acceptance technique with her. At first, it was difficult for her to hear what I was saying because she wanted to get back with Steve so badly. She did not understand how accepting him as he is would help her. Also, she was afraid that accepting him meant condoning the qualities in him that bothered her, and she could not do that. So I told

her to pretend that Steve had two heads and that, although she wanted a guy with only one head, Steve had two—and it was not possible to cut one of them off. She either had to accept that he had two heads or let him go. That example clicked and she understood it! She instantly changed before my eyes! She stopped crying, she sat up straight, her eyes got clear and she glowed.

A few days later, Sally and Steve talked. Steve was very critical of Sally and shared what was on his mind. For the first time in their relationship, Sally was able to listen to Steve without reacting defensively. Because she had accepted him as he is, she understood him and where he was coming from. This was a miracle! Sally and Steve are now able to resume their relationship because she is no longer critical of him. In fact, she is able to see good qualities in him she never recognized before! In addition, Steve's refusal to consider marriage is no longer an issue between them. They are taking it one step at a time.

Sally says that she is totally transformed, and now uses the acceptance technique on all the people and situations in her life. One of her biggest issues was her relationship with her children, particularly her daughter. Sally was always outgoing and popular in school, and had lots of friends. She wanted her daughter to be the same way. However, while her daughter was popular, she was also very shy, quiet and introverted. Sally's disappointment and criticism of her daughter created problems between them for years. Now, though, as a result of the acceptance technique, she no longer wants her daughter to change. She sees her daughter through new eyes, and their relationship has completely turned around.

Sally feels a freedom she has never felt before. She recognizes the power of the acceptance technique and is so grateful to know about it. She agrees with one of my students who said, "Acceptance doesn't solve the problem—it eliminates it."

Powerful stuff.

How to Discover
Your Commitments

There are 7 major commitments you made as a child. These commitments form the foundation of your story. They were created sequentially, one at a time:

1) Your commitment to your mother
2) Your commitment to your father
3) Your commitment to your family
4) Your commitment to your original team (your family team)
5) Your commitment to your original spouse (your

family spouse)

6) Your commitment to your childhood self (your ego)
7) Your commitment to your original child (your family child)

Because these commitments build on one another, you release them in the order in which you made them. After you release a commitment, you rewrite it your way and accept it. Actually, what you are doing is creating a new commitment to yourself about your mother, father, family, etc. Once you discover your original commitments, your story will be clear to you, and you will be able to rewrite it the way you want it to be.

There is a very simple way to uncover your commitments, which you can do alone or with a supportive friend. Your first commitment is to your mother, so let's use her as our example.

Make a list of everything you were supposed to do, be or have to make her happy. This could include getting good grades, taking care of your baby brother, being seen and not heard, or whatever comes to mind. Once you have your list, allow yourself to feel what you have written. If you are working with a buddy, talk about how you are feeling. If you are working by yourself, you might want to pretend you are with a trusted friend and talk out loud, as if the friend were present.

As you talk, one (or more) of the items on your list will jump out at you. As you zoom in on it and talk about it, you will feel it more deeply, and you will actually say the words that describe your commitment. These are the words that resonate with you. You will know they are right because they will *feel* right. No one has to agree with you. This is *your* commitment, and you will recognize the right words when you feel them.

Your list might look something like this:

- Smile and be courteous to everyone
- Dry the dinner dishes
- Dust the house
- Take care of your younger sister
- Control your younger brother and keep him from misbehaving in public
- Be a good child
- Make A's in school
- Be an adult
- Be independent
- Figure out your homework by yourself
- Keep the family secrets

As you begin talking about the list and getting in touch with your feelings about it, the pieces of the puzzle will start to come together. It may become very clear, for example, that your commitment to your mother was to **be her helper**.

Once again, you will know this is right because it *feels* right.

When you have identified your original commitment to your mother, use the releasing technique to let it go by saying:

"Dear God (or the words that describe God to you), I totally release my original commitment to my mother to _____ to you." Then release the commitment.

After you release the original commitment you made to your mother as a child, rewrite it as you would like it to be. Since this is really your commitment to yourself about your mother, say what you would like to say to her, even if she is no longer living. This new statement is your new commitment to your mother. Use the acceptance technique to accept it by saying,

"I totally accept my new commitment to my mother to _____." Then accept your new commitment.

Accept the following declarations one by one as well:

"I totally accept my mother just as she is."
"I totally accept that I am in charge of my life."
"I totally accept that I am responsible for my happiness."
"I totally accept that I am free to think for myself."

You are now ready to release your original commitment to your father, and the rest of the commitments in sequential order.

Your Commitment
To Your Mother

Your first commitment is to your mother.

Your mother is the most important person in your life, and your commitment to her is the strongest commitment of all. It sets the tone for all your subsequent commitments.

Your mother carries you in her body for nine months. Her cells become your cells; her emotions become your emotions; her thoughts, your thoughts; her fears, your fears. If she thinks she is smart, you not only think she is smart, you think *you* are smart, too. If she thinks she is valuable, you think, so too, and you think *you* are valuable as well. If she has low self esteem, so do you. In other words, you think like your mother.

Even after you are born and the umbilical cord is cut, the emotional cord remains. Even if she is no longer living, your commitment to her is alive and well. It is in your cells; it is part of you and controls you until you see it, let it go and rewrite it.

Keep in mind that you made this commitment on the heels of your Bad Message, your first conscious trauma. This commitment was your unspoken agreement, your bargain with her. Implicit in this agreement was the hope of getting good enough to return to the proverbial Garden of Eden, where you were the center of her life, unconditionally loved and, above all, good. In addition you hoped that she would give you her permission to move forward without her into the world.

If you disobey, rebel and refuse to live up to your commitment, you risk never regaining her unconditional love, never being good, and never returning to the Garden of Eden. In other words, not being loved, remaining bad and living in emotional hell. This is unthinkable, and this fear is what keeps you locked into your commitment. On some level, you think you can get good enough to change things and return to the way they were when you were a child. This is not possible.

The way to change things is to move forward. You do this by recognizing that your obedience to or rebellion against this commitment has not worked, and that it is up to you to let go of your commitment to your mother and replace it with a new one that you consciously create.

Some astute students have asked whether we make the new commitment to our mother or to ourselves. Powerful, insightful question!

You actually write your new commitment to yourself about your mother. In the next chapter, when you write your new commitment to your father, you actually write your new commitment to yourself about your father. You do this with each commitment. This is how you consciously rewrite your story. And since this is *your* commitment, you can write it any way you want.

> I learned this from Steven, a handsome young man in his early 40s. Even as a child, he had tried to get his mother to end her relationships with abusive men. She did not listen to him. When he was older, he actually got into a fight with one of her boyfriends for abusing her. She still did not listen to him.
>
> When Steven identified and released his original commitment to his mother and was ready to write his new commitment to her, he asked me, "Can I just say I don't owe her a damn thing?"
>
> My response was, "If that's how you feel, absolutely!"
>
> He then accepted his new commitment to his mother (his commitment to himself about his mother), which was, **"I don't owe you a damn thing!"**

In addition to your birth mother, you may have a stepmother

or an adoptive mother. It may be that another relative filled the role of mother in your life. If this describes your childhood, you have made a commitment to each of them, and you will want to discover, release and rewrite your commitment to each mother figure separately. Simply do the releasing and acceptance technique with each of them as well as your birth mother.

Your Original Commitment to Your Mother

After you have made a list of how you had to make your mother happy, boil it down to one sentence or phrase and say:

"Dear God (or the words that describe God to you), I totally release my original commitment to my mother to _____ *to you."* Then release the commitment.

Your New Commitment to Your Mother

After you have written your new commitment to your mother (your commitment to yourself about your mother), say:

"Dear God (or the words that describe God to you), I totally accept my new commitment to my mother to _____.*"* Then accept your new commitment.

Accept the following declarations one by one as well:

"I totally accept my mother just as she is."
"I totally accept that I am in charge of my life."
"I totally accept that I am responsible for my happiness."
"I totally accept that I am free to think for myself."

Your Commitment
To Your Father

Your second commitment is to your father, the second most important person in your life.

We often turn to him to give us what our mother could not: attention, love, guidance, etc.

Your father teaches you how to act out the in the world. You watch him and act like him. You do things the way he does. You may even follow in his career footsteps. You learn how to interact with others by imitating him. You want his approval, and your commitment to him reflects this.

> Ray is excellent at home repairs and has earned
> a wonderful reputation as a professional home
> repairman. Ray's son, Dave, began accompanying
> his father on jobs as soon as he was old enough to
> do so, and learned at his father's feet. Today, Dave
> is also in great demand as a professional home
> repairman.

If your father is extroverted and loves people, you will interact
with people the same way. If your father is serious and aloof
when he first meets people, you will be serious and aloof as
well. If your father is generous, you, too, will be generous; if
he is critical, you, too, will be critical.

In a little girl's life, her father sets the tone for her relationships
with other men. She observes how he treats her mother, and
this determines the kind of relationship she will have with
the men in her life. Unknowingly, she may attract someone
like her father. If her father is verbally abusive, that is the
kind of man she will attract; if he is affectionate and loving,
that is the kind of man she will attract.

> When Helen was three years old, her baby sister was
> born. Her mother gave the baby all her attention,
> and Helen felt rejected and unloved. She turned to
> her father for the love she needed. Her father was
> closed, unhappy and unaffectionate, and that is
> how Helen learned to act. She emulated her father
> and built a wall around herself just as he taught
> her to do. During her teens and 20s, she was not
> attracted to open, happy, outgoing men. Instead,

she was drawn to men just like her father.

It was not until Helen let go of her original commitment to **make her father her god** that she was able to let down her wall and express the love she felt for people.

Just as with little girls, a little boy watches the interaction between his parents. This tells him how to treat women. If his father treats his mother with respect and love, this is how he will treat women; if his father puts his career ahead of his wife and family, this is what the little boy will do when he grows up.

In addition to your birth father, you may have a stepfather or an adoptive father. It may be that another relative filled the role of father in your life. If this describes your childhood, you have made a commitment to each of them, and you will want to discover, release and rewrite your commitment to each father figure separately. Simply do the releasing and acceptance technique with each of them as well as your birth father.

Your Original Commitment to Your Father

After you have made a list of what you had to do to make your father happy, boil it down to one sentence or phrase and say:

"Dear God (or the words that describe God to you), I totally release my original commitment to my father to _____ *to you."* Then release it.

Your New Commitment to Your Father

After you have written your new commitment to your father (your commitment to yourself about your father), say:

"Dear God (or the words that describe God to you), I totally accept my new commitment to my father to _____."
Then accept your new commitment.

Accept the following declarations one by one as well:

"I totally accept my father just as he is."
"I totally accept that I am God's child." (Or, "I totally accept that I am a child of the universe.")
"I totally accept that I am free to do things my way and act the way I want."

Your Commitment
To Your Family

✳

Your third commitment is to your family.

Your family tells you how they want you to be, and your commitment to them reflects your desire to be that way in order to gain their acceptance.

While families consist of brothers, sisters, grandparents, aunts, uncles, and cousins, this commitment is usually made to siblings.

If you were an only child, you may consider your parents to

be your family. Or, if your cousins were close to you, you may see them as your family. Maybe your grandparents helped raise you, in which case they may be the ones who represent family to you.

> Nancy, an insightful student of human nature, had an interesting, though not uncommon, family dynamic. Her mother and sister had such a tight, impenetrable, exclusive bond, that Nancy could not think of one without the other. She considered these two joined-at-the-hip people to be her family, and it was to them that she made her commitment.

Some people make their original commitment to their entire family.

> Gary's immediate family consisted of his parents and two older sisters. His commitment to each of them was different. To one sister, he was to be her confidant and keep her secrets; to another, he was to be her baby brother; to his father, he was to be a star athlete; to his mother he was to be "a good boy". All of them expected him to excel at whatever he did. The pressure to live up to these commitments caused him to drop out of college for a year.

> Gary could not focus on just one family member, but saw all of them as his family. As we talked and he shared the expectations placed on him, it became clear that his commitment to his family was to **be a super star**.

If you have any trouble identifying who represents your family to you, just start talking about all the people who might fall into this category. As you talk, one will stand out from the rest and you will know that they are the relative who represents your family to you.

Your Original Commitment to Your Family

After you have made a list of how you had to be in order to make your family happy, boil it down to one sentence or phrase and say:

"Dear God (or the words that describe God to you), I totally release my original commitment to my family to _____ to you." Then release the commitment.

Your New Commitment to Your Family

After you have written your new commitment to your family (your commitment to yourself about your family), say:

"Dear God (or the words that describe God to you), I totally accept my new commitment to my family to _____."
Then accept your new commitment.

Accept the following declarations one by one as well:

"I totally accept my family just as it is."
"I totally accept that I am the Spirit that is, was and always will be."
"I totally accept that I am free to be the way I want."

Your Commitment To Your Family Team

Your fourth commitment is to your original team: your family team.

Once you make your original commitments to your mother, father and family, the pattern of your life is set. From then on, you take your commitments out into the world and unknowingly transfer them onto the people with whom you interact: your friends, co-workers, bosses, spouses, children, pets, and even strangers.

This means that if someone upsets you, all you have to do to clarify the situation is ask yourself, "Is this person showing me my mother, father or family?" By simply identifying which family member this person represents, the pieces fall into place, you see your story with greater clarity, and the pain of the current situation is greatly diminished.

You can belong to many teams, such as work teams, religious teams, sports teams, in-law teams, school teams, etc. However, your first team is your family team. Your family team makes the rules for your life and tells you what you can and cannot have. Your place on your original family team determines your place in the world with all your teams. Your story with your original family team is repeated with all the others.

Think of which family member made the rules for your life and told you what you can or cannot have, and you will be able to identify your original team. You may find that more than one family member falls into this category.

> Sandy's original team was her brother, who controlled their mother by yelling and demanding to have his way. From the time she was little, Sandy knew that her job was to put her brother first and give him whatever he wanted in every area of life. Sandy saw that her commitment to her original brother team was to **get it and give it to him.** This played out in all her relationships.
>
> After releasing her commitment to her brother team, Sandy saw that because she is a hard worker, she has always been able to recoup and reclaim her losses. This opened her eyes. Now she is free

to keep what she gets. She jokingly said that she is ready to win the lottery—and keep it!

Your Original Commitment to Your Family Team

After you have identified your family team and made a list of what you had to do to make your family team happy, boil it down to one sentence or phrase and say:

"Dear God (or the words that describe God to you), I totally release my original commitment to my family team to _____ to you." Then release the commitment.

Your New Commitment to Your Family Team

After you have written your new commitment to your family team (your commitment to yourself about your family), say:

"Dear God (or the words that describe God to you), I totally accept my new commitment to my family team to _____." Then accept your new commitment.

Accept the following declarations one by one as well:

"I totally accept my family team just as it is."
"I totally accept that I am the creator of my life."
"I totally accept that I am free to have what I want."

Your Commitment To Your Family Spouse

✳

Your fifth commitment is to your family spouse. Just as you have an original family team, you have an original family spouse.

This is not a literal spousal relationship, but an emotional bond you have with the family member you rely on. Your relationship with your family spouse can prevent you from finding an actual adult spouse. Or, if you are able to marry, because you are still emotionally married to your original family spouse, it may be difficult to be truly committed to the person you have chosen to be your spouse, which can cause problems in your marriage.

Nina, a very successful businesswoman in her 30s, complained that she wants to get married and have children, but continues to attract men who are poorly suited to her. She has had a few long term relationships, but none of them have led to marriage.

When I asked her about her father, she told me that she adores him, talks to him daily, and seeks his advice on everything. They are best friends. This is the problem: she already has a man in her life (her father), so the husband slot is already taken. In addition, no man can compare with her perfect father spouse.

Barbara's son is an attractive, outgoing, businessman in his 40s. He is straight, eligible, and, while he has dated many women, he has remained single. Barbara says she would love to see him get married and raise a family. As we talked about their relationship, she told me that she has always been there for him. She has let him live with her and has helped him out financially on several occasions. They are friends as well as parent and child. They talk regularly and she has always treated him as the man in her life. Why would he look for another woman? He has already found the perfect wife: his mother.

To find out who your family spouse is, ask yourself which family member you relied on growing up and whom you may still be relying on as an adult. This will help you identify the family member to whom you are emotionally married. Incidentally, your family spouse can be the same sex you are or the opposite sex. Their gender is not the important part; your reliance on them is.

Your Original Commitment to Your Family Spouse

After you have identified your family spouse and made a list of what you had to do to make him or her happy, boil it down to one sentence or phrase and say:

"Dear God (or the words that describe God to you), I totally release my original commitment to my family spouse to _____ to you." Then release the commitment.

Your New Commitment to Your Family Spouse

After you have written your new commitment to your family spouse (your commitment to yourself about your family spouse), say:

"Dear God (or the words that describe God to you), I totally accept my new commitment to my family spouse to _____." Then accept your new commitment.

Accept the following declarations one by one as well:

"I totally accept my family spouse just as he or she is."
"I totally accept that I rely on the Spirit (God) within me."
"I totally accept that I am free to rely on myself."

Your Commitment
To Your Ego

✳

Your sixth commitment is your commitment to your childhood self, your ego.

The ego is a false creation of the mind. It is not who you are, but it is who you *think* you are and who you tell the world you are. Because it is not real, your ego needs others to tell it who it is and give it feedback.

The ego is filled with doubt, fear and insecurity. It needs constant proof that it is right and, just like a child, it wants what it wants when it wants it. The ego needs constant attention and recognition, and gets hurt and angry if it does not get what it wants. We all know people who monopolize the conversation and have to be center stage at all times. It is their ego that demands the limelight and wants to be heard.

We have all been with grown men and women who still act like children and require our undivided attention. Like a child with its mother, they show off their "toys" and brag about their accomplishments.

> Matt is a brilliant, retired businessman who had a highly successful career. He is outgoing, generous, and makes friends wherever he goes. However, he requires the undivided attention of whoever he is with. If you ask him a question, he launches into a detailed story designed to hold your attention for as long as possible, and if you disagree with him or question him, he becomes impatient and angry. If you bring up a subject, you can actually feel him waiting for you to pause for breath so he can jump in, grab the conversation and run with it. His ego must have the limelight.

> Brittany saw that if she does something that displeases someone else, and they raise their voice and act like a parent, she (her ego) moves into the role of reprimanded child and feels guilty, not good enough, and pitiful. She covers this up with self-righteous anger. In reality, she is embarrassed, humiliated and ashamed of herself, and cannot face the other person, so she pulls away from

them. The truth is that she (her ego) is punishing herself for having made a mistake, and pulls back in the hopes that the other person will come after her and forgive her.

While some people are genuinely quiet, gentle, and caring, and do not need or want to be the center of attention, others disguise their ego behind a façade of humility and silence. This ego still wants the attention, but has learned to attract it by being less obvious. And some people believe that they are so worthless that they do not deserve any attention at all. This ego wants no attention.

The childish ego keeps you from expressing your innate gifts, talents and abilities. When you let go of this original commitment and rewrite it, you are free to express your True Self.

Your Original Commitment to Your Ego

After you have made a list of what you had to do for your ego, boil it down to one sentence or phrase and say:

"Dear God (or the words that describe God to you), I totally release my original commitment to my ego to _____ to you." Then release the commitment.

Your New Commitment to Your Ego

After you have written your new commitment to your True Self (your commitment to yourself about yourself), say:

"Dear God (or the words that describe God to you), I totally accept my new commitment to my True Self to _____."
Then accept your new commitment.

Accept the following declarations one by one as well:

"I totally accept myself just as I am."
"I totally accept that my True Self is Spirit (God) in physical form."
"I totally accept that I am free to say what I want and express my True Self."

Your Commitment
To Your Family
Child

Your seventh commitment is to your family child. In addition to a family team and a family spouse, you have a family child.

This is the person you nurture, protect and take care of. It can be a parent, sibling or other relative, or it can be more than one person.

The family member who is your original child determines how you will take care of people out in the world, and describes the type of person who will turn to you for nurturing.

This commitment to your family child keeps you from having fun and enjoying yourself because, as a surrogate parent, you have the responsibility for the health, safety and well-being of your "child". This inappropriate responsibility is given to you, either verbally or nonverbally, by a parent. It frees them to handle other areas of their life, but it can rob you of your own childhood.

> When Susan was little, she loved babies. However, when her brother was born, Susan's mother gave her the role of big sister = surrogate mother. Her brother was difficult to manage and required more and more attention. The more attention her brother required, the more responsibility Susan was given as the big sister. The more responsibility she was given, the less she liked children until, as an adult, she resented them and made the conscious decision not to have any of her own.

> It was only after Susan released her original commitment to her brother child that she was able to recapture and express her childhood love for babies. This grew and expanded to include everyone.

To identify your family child, ask yourself who you were supposed to nurture, and who prevented you from having fun. This can be anyone in your original family, and it can be more than one person.

Your Original Commitment to Your Family Child

After you have identified your family child and made a list of what you had to do to take care of him or her, boil it down to one sentence or phrase and say:

"Dear God (or the words that describe God to you), I totally release my original commitment to my family child to _____ to you." Then release the commitment.

Your New Commitment to Your Family Child

After you have written your new commitment to your family child (your commitment to yourself about your family child), say:

"Dear God (or the words that describe God to you), I totally accept my new commitment to my family child to _____." Then accept your new commitment.

Accept the following declarations one by one as well:

"I totally accept my family child just as he or she is."
"I totally accept that I am free to have fun and enjoy myself."

Peggi's Story

✴

Peggi's Commitment to Her Mother

Peggi's Original Commitment to Her Mother

Peggi's original commitment to her strict, religious mother was to **be good, be quiet, and do what she was told**. What this meant was that she was to do God's will and not have a will of her own. Her mother was the vehicle through which God operated, so if she disobeyed her mother, she was disobeying God. Peggi was a rebellious child, and her parents took turns beating her in order to get her to obey them/God. When her mother realized she could not force Peggi to be obedient, she changed tactics and used guilt.

As a child, Peggi always asked herself, "Is this something that God wants me to do or is Satan trying to trick me into doing what *he* wants me to do?" As she grew up, her confusion grew. In order to function within the rules of her religious family and community, she learned to live a double life and put on a façade in order to appear to be perfect.

Peggi's New Commitment to Her Mother

After letting go of her original commitment to her mother, Peggi wrote and accepted her new commitment: **"I love and accept my mother as she is—and I live my own life."**

Peggi's Commitment to Her Father

Peggi's Original Commitment to Her Father

Peggi's father wanted her to be his confidante, his companion and to keep his secrets. He would often tell her things he did not want her mother to know. He was bipolar and, as he got older, was simply unable to work, so Peggi helped out financially for a time.

Her original commitment to her father was to **have his back.** This meant keeping her mother happy, which kept her off *his* back.

Peggi's New Commitment to Her Father

"I'm not responsible for you."

Peggi's Commitment to Her Family

Peggi's Original Commitment to Her Family

Peggi considered her grandfather and her siblings to be her family. When Peggi was little, she was the apple of her grandfather's eye, and they adored one another. He took care of her, and she went everywhere with him. Her original commitment to him was to **be his helpmate**.

Peggi's New Commitment to Her Grandfather

"I'm just fine the way I am."

When Peggi was six, her grandfather died. She no longer had anyone to take care of her, and she felt lost, confused and alone. Like many people who do not receive or stop receiving the nurturing they need, she *gave* nurturing and became the family nurturer. As she got older and her younger sister and brother were born, she became their **surrogate mother**. This was her original commitment to them. Neither of her parents was emotionally capable of nurturing, so Peggi looked out for her siblings and cared for them.

While Peggi has broken free from the restrictive, fundamental religion in which she was raised and is now able to see the truth and think her own thoughts, her siblings have not, and are still very involved in their church. In order to maintain a close relationship with one another, they have a don't-ask-don't-tell family dynamic.

Peggi's New Commitment to Her Siblings

"I love you, and we all have to lead our own lives."

Peggi's Commitment to Her Family Team

Peggi's Original Commitment to Her Family Team

When Peggi's grandfather died, she felt he had abandoned her. She was still part of her family, but did not feel included. Two years later, when Peggi was eight, her sister was born. From then on, she felt pushed aside and abandoned by her mother. In order to feel included in her family, Peggi became the caretaker. As she grew up, this extended to any group with which she was involved. She learned very early to smile and get people to talk about themselves so she would not have to worry about what to say. Her family team's message to her was: **do not be seen and do not be heard**. This was her original commitment to them and explains why she had always felt invisible.

As we talked about her life, she told me that her grandmother, who was very active in the church, had held the lease to her parents' home, which her grandfather had built. As long as her grandmother was alive, Peggi's family could live in their house. However, when she died, the family had the fear of eviction hanging over their heads. And, in fact, the owner finally *did* ask them to move.

The other very important team for most of Peggi's life was her church team. This team told her she **could not have anything or anyone**, and that was her original commitment to them.

As a child, she could not be part of "worldly" teams, just her church team, so she never learned how to get along in the world. She says she was never socialized. Recently she has started seeing that she is liked and that people want to be her friend.

Peggi's New Commitment to Her Family Team

"I'm here and I'm an important part of the group. I can't change or fix you—and I am liked!"

Peggi's Commitment to Her Family Spouse

Peggi's Original Commitment to Her Family Spouse

Peggi's original spouse was her grandfather. They adored one another. He was a builder and carpenter, and she would go with him when he worked to hand him his tools and supplies. Her original commitment to her grandfather spouse was to **do his will, please him and adore him**. She relied on him for love and attention, but he died when she was six, and left her with no one to rely on. Her father then became her spouse, but he was emotionally and mentally unavailable. Her grandfather was married to her grandmother, and her father was married to her mother, so she could not really have them. She has continued this pattern with her husband, who has abandoned her to his own interests. Her original commitment to her grandfather spouse and father spouse was to **have him and not have him, then lose him**.

Peggi's New Commitment to Her Family Spouses

"Live your own life; I'm living mine."

Peggi's Commitment to Her Ego

Peggi's Original Commitment to Her Ego

Peggi always felt less than everyone else. Her religious upbringing taught her that she was not important and should not have anything. She was supposed to sacrifice and deprive herself of what she wanted. Her original commitment to her ego was **to sacrifice herself to show how good she is**.

Peggi's New Commitment to Her True Self

"Peggi, you can have anything you want, and I love and care for you."

Peggi's Commitment to Her Family Children

Peggi's Original Commitment to Her Family Children

When Peggi was growing up, she took on the role of nurturer in order to survive, and took care of her parents, her brother and her sister. They had very little money and often, so little food, that they ate mush. Her parents were in the church ministry and believed that God (the church) would take care of them. However, it was Peggi who, as a young adult, stepped in when needed, whether emotionally or financially. They were all her children, and her original commitment to them was **to make their world okay, to keep them safe, and to make them happy**.

Peggi's New Commitment to Her Family Children

"Live and let live."

Today, Peggi is at the brink of fully living her mission, and cannot wait to move forward full throttle.

Loren's Story

Loren's Commitment to Her Mother

Loren's Original Commitment to Her Mother

From the time that she was a child, Loren and her mother reversed roles. Loren took on the role of mother, and her mother took on the role of child. A mother, traditionally, builds her life around her child, and that is what Loren did with her mother. Whenever they got together, they always talked about her mother and her mother's issues, not Loren's. As Loren said, "It was always about her."

On one recent occasion, Loren's doctor found a disturbing mark on her mammogram, so she made a follow up appointment. When she told her mother about the appointment, her mother offered to come with her, which was lovely. In the next breath, she said to Loren, "But I know you won't want me to come with you because you don't like me." Even when Loren needed her mother most, her mother brought the situation back to herself.

Loren was to let her mother have the success and happiness that she, herself, wanted. Loren was supposed to be her friend and keep the family secrets. Loren's mother depended on her for her own emotional survival, for which Loren felt responsible. Her original commitment to her mother was **to make her mother her life and to give up her life for her mother**.

Loren's New Commitment to Her Mother

To be completely committed to her own life, her own mission and her own joy.

Loren's Commitment to Her Father

Loren's Original Commitment to Her Father

When Loren moved back home with her parents because of financial problems she was having, she slept on a bed in her father's small home office. Although she had always had lots of boyfriends and, in fact, had been married and divorced, marriage and children were not what she wanted. This was because her original commitment to her father was **to be his partner**, which did not leave room for another man. She was to be there for him, and not the other way around.

Loren's New Commitment to Her Father

"I give him back to my mother, and leave the door open for the right and perfect partner to come to me."

Loren's Commitment to Her Family

Loren's Original Commitment to Her Family

Loren is the oldest of five siblings. Even as a child, she took care of them and was their baby sitter. As we talked, she focused on one of her brothers, who has been a success in life. She was to sacrifice for her family, just as a mother would, and let her brother have the success and happiness that she, herself, wanted. It was always about her siblings, not her. Her original commitment to her family was to **be their surrogate mother**.

Loren's New Commitment to Her Family

"I take care of my own needs first, and reclaim my life and my childhood. I am a living, breathing example to the world of the healing power and joy of loving the self."

Loren's Commitment to Her Family Team

Loren's Original Commitment to Her Family Team

Her role as surrogate mother continued with her family team, and was represented by one of her younger brothers. Her original commitment to him was **to protect him and act as a buffer between him and their parents so that he could have the love, success and family she could never have.**

Loren's New Commitment to Her Family Team

To completely and fully reclaim all that she could not have and could not be, and to be the successful celebrity she was born to be.

Loren's Commitment to Her Family Spouse

Loren's Original Commitment to Her Family Spouse

Loren's original spouse was her father. And just as her mother expected him to take care of her financially, so did Loren. She transferred this to the other men in her life, and she verbalized her original commitment to her father spouse this way: **"I am what he and all men want me to be (partner, surrogate mother) so that they'll take care of me."**

Loren's New Commitment to Her Family Spouse

"To fully and completely take care of myself, wonderfully and grandly, so that I can choose to love and give without an agenda."

✶

Loren's Commitment to Her Ego

Loren's Original Commitment to Her Ego

"To give myself nothing and spite myself however I can. One day I'll get revenge on all of them and then die. That will make them feel sorry."

Loren's New Commitment to Her True Self

"To have everything I've ever wanted. To allow and have my deepest dreams come true, and to fully and deeply enjoy my life."

✶

Loren's Commitment to Her Family Child

Loren's Original Commitment to Her Family Child

Loren's original child was her mother, with whom she reversed roles. Just as a mother does, Loren put all her attention on her mother, to the exclusion of herself and her own needs. Her maternal role then expanded to include her father, her siblings and the entire world. Her original commitment to her surrogate children, starting with her mother, was "**to give them everything I've got and take care of their needs before my own. To put their lives before my own and give up my life for their lives.**"

Loren's New Commitment to Her Family Children

To kick them out of the nest and let them live their own lives. "I'm leaving now to live my own life. Good-bye."

Loren's role as surrogate mother runs through her original commitments and tells the story of her life.

Today, Loren has her own apartment, a new job, a new car, and is applying for doctoral programs. She is creating the life *she* wants to live.

Marilyn's Story

✳

Marilyn's Commitment to Her Mother

Marilyn's Original Commitment to Her Mother

Marilyn knew exactly what her original commitment to her mother was. It was **to make her happy**. This meant solving any problem that might upset her mother, no matter what it was or who it was with. To do this, she became proactive, vigilant, and anticipated problems before they surfaced. She spent her life putting out fires and solving everyone's problems (before they got to her mother and upset her), to the exclusion of her own.

When she was little, her mother cried a lot because Marilyn's brother is mentally ill and one of her sisters was on drugs. As a result, Marilyn made up her mind that she would never hurt her mother the way her brother and sister did, and became the "good" child to make up for the "bad" ones.

Marilyn's New Commitment to Her Mother

Marilyn's parents, who are in their 80s, moved close to where she lives, and she is really enjoying being with them. Her new commitment to her mother is **to enjoy her while her mother is here and recognize that she is not responsible for making her mother happy**.

Marilyn's Commitment to Her Father

Marilyn's Original Commitment to Her Father

While Marilyn adored her mother, she feared her strict, angry father. He was the baby who ruled the roost. However, he hated to see his wife cry. If his wife was happy, he was happy. So Marilyn's original commitment to her father was to **save her mother and do whatever it took to make her happy**. But, in order to make her mother happy, Marilyn had to **take care of everyone and everything**. This was her true commitment to her father.

Marilyn's New Commitment to Her Father

Marilyn is so grateful her parents are alive and living nearby so she can enjoy them. Her new commitment to her father is **to enjoy him without taking care of him and the whole family**.

Marilyn's Commitment to Her Family

Marilyn's Original Commitment to Her Family

Marilyn is the middle child in a family of one brother and three sisters, two of whom are still extremely needy. Because of her original commitments to her parents, she always took care of everyone in her family, and they came to expect it. She became a master at solving everyone's problems and fixing things. Growing up, the household was filled with yelling, shouting and crying, and her attention was always on everyone else rather than on herself. She was not supposed to need them, but she *was* supposed to be there when they needed *her*. Her original commitment to her family was **to make everyone happy and solve all their problems without needing them or anything from them**.

Marilyn's New Commitment to Her Family

Marilyn has changed the rules. She no longer acts as a go between when her sisters have a problem. Her new commitment to her family is **to enjoy each of them without feeling obligated or guilty for not solving their problems or taking care of them**.

Marilyn's Commitment to Her Family Team

Marilyn's Original Commitment to Her Family Team

Marilyn's entire family was her original team. Her siblings are all different, and so are her friends. However, she sees that, just as her siblings are needy, so are her closest friends. She is funny and entertaining in order to keep them happy, just as she was with her family. Her original commitment to her family team was **to make them all happy by being available for them, solving their problems and being a sounding board**.

Marilyn's New Commitment to Her Family Team

It is no surprise that Marilyn's new commitment to her family team and friendship team is **to enjoy their friendship without obligation**.

Marilyn's Commitment to Her Family Spouse

Marilyn's Original Commitment to Her Family Spouse

Marilyn's mother was her original spouse. She was the only person Marilyn trusted and the only one who gave her unconditional love. Her original commitment to her mother spouse was **to always be there for her**.

Marilyn's New Commitment to Her Family Spouse

Marilyn's mother is happy when Marilyn is happy, so Marilyn's new commitment to her mother spouse is **to be happy with herself as she is**.

Marilyn's Commitment to Her Ego

Marilyn's Original Commitment to Her Ego

Even when Marilyn was little, she felt like an adult because she was expected to be one. She never had a childhood. Her original commitment to her ego was **to be responsible for everyone**.

Marilyn's New Commitment to Her True Self

Today, Marilyn's commitment to her True Self is **to enjoy life**.

Marilyn's Commitment to Her Family Child

Marilyn's Original Commitment to Her Family Child

Marilyn's sister Barbara is two years her junior. When Barbara was born, she became Marilyn's child. Barbara was and is very emotionally and physically needy. Marilyn's original commitment to Barbara was **to take care of her, which meant giving her whatever she needed**.

Marilyn's New Commitment to Her Family Child

Marilyn has enabled Barbara and exhausted herself by solving her problems for her since she was a baby. Her new commitment to Barbara is **to let her be a grown up now**.

Recently, Marilyn did something totally out of character: she left her high-paying, stress-filled job because she was burned out. This gave her the freedom to enjoy her parents, her husband and her daughter. She is learning to have fun and take time for herself.

Hope's Story

✳

Hope's Commitment to Her Mother

Hope's Original Commitment to Her Mother

Hope and her mother have always been close. She was her mother's friend, child and parent. She gave up her childhood and, subsequently, her life, for her mother, and protected her from her father, a mean, angry alcoholic. Part of this protection included protecting her two brothers as well.

Hope's original commitment to her mother was "**to be her protector and make her the center of my life.**"

Hope's New Commitment to Her Mother

Hope is still close to her mother and family, but is now taking a stand for herself. Her new commitment to her mother is, "*I am my world.*"

Hope's Commitment to Her Father

Hope's Original Commitment to Her Father

Hope's father was popular with his friends, but mean to his family. He was always angry, probably because he was always drunk. No matter what she did, Hope was never good enough in her father's eyes. She did not count and did not have a voice or a role in his life. She could be seen, but not heard. To him, Hope did not exist. Her original commitment to her father was to **never be good enough, and to be his verbal and emotional punching bag**.

Hope's New Commitment to Her Father

One of the strongest messages from her father was that she was not great or fabulous and neither were her children. Her new commitment to her father is, **"I am great, I am fabulous and so are my kids. I won't give my kids the same messages you gave me."**

Hope's Commitment to Her Family

Hope's Original Commitment to Her Family

Hope was the surrogate mother to her family, which consisted of her parents and two brothers. She was the adult who took care of everyone else and gave them what they wanted. When her children were very small, and Hope had to go out into the world and earn a living in order to support them, she hired one of her brothers to babysit during the day. This was win/win. Now that her children are older, they no longer need a babysitter.

Growing up, Hope was abused and taken advantage of. Her original commitment to her family, **to be the adult**, tells it all. This commitment set the tone for her interactions out in the world.

Hope's New Commitment to Her Family

Hope's new commitment to her family illustrates how far she has come: **"I will no longer be used. I won't be bound. I am cherished and adored, respected, appreciated and treated with love."**

Hope's Commitment to Her Family Team

Hope's Original Commitment to Her Family Team

Our teams tell us what we can have. Hope's original team was her mother, and her mother was the only one she could have. Hope felt that she was born to protect her. She could not have more than her mother had; she could not surpass her. This expanded to include everyone on her family team. As a surrogate mother, she did not have a childhood. She could not have a voice or be outspoken.

At one point in her childhood, she was so unhappy that she begged to please go live with her grandmother, who was suffering from cancer. She preferred living with a sick grandmother to living with her family. Her request was denied because she was to stay home and protect the family, which protected her mother. Another time, she begged to go to boarding school. Again, she was turned down for the same reason.

Hope's original commitment to her family team was **to put up and shut up, and make everyone else look good**.

Hope's New Commitment to Her Family Team

One of her father's messages was, "You have no value unless you're a success." How can you succeed if you cannot speak or be seen? If you cannot have what you want?

Hope's new commitment to her family team is, **"I am valued and appreciated, and I can have it all."**

Hope's Commitment to Her Family Spouse

Hope's Original Commitment to Her Family Spouse

Hope's mother was her original spouse. One of their

agreements was that Hope would protect her mother's reputation. What this meant was that Hope was to keep the family secrets and not let the world know that her father was a drunk or her brother was in jail again.

Hope's original commitment to her mother spouse was to **be there for her, and protect her and her reputation**.

Hope's New Commitment to Her Family Spouse

It is interesting that Hope's new commitment to her mother spouse is a repeat of her new commitment to her mother: **"_I_ am my world."**

Hope's Commitment to Her Ego

Hope's Original Commitment to Her Ego

Hope was supposed to be needed. This was where she got her worth and value. It explains, also, why she went into nursing as a career, and why she attracted needy people—so she could fix them.

Her original commitment to her ego was, **"Everyone else is first. Being needed is the only value I have. Fix everyone."**

Hope's New Commitment to Her True Self

Hope's new commitment shows that she has broken free from the caretaker role: **"I'm first, I'm valued and I have healthy people in my life."**

Hope's Commitment to Her Family Child

Hope's Original Commitment to Her Family Child

Hope said that she never had fun as a child because she reversed roles with her mother, and her mother became *her* child. Her original commitment to her mother child was **to take care of her in every way. Be her parent, friend, confidante and companion, and make her happy.**

Hope's New Commitment to Her Family Child

Hope gave up her childhood in order to devote her life to her mother. Her new commitment to her mother child is: **"I take back me. I can have fun. I will not do to my own daughter what my mother did to me."**

Today, Hope has a wonderful new job where she is appreciated and respected, and an active social life. She is still close with her family, but she is living her new commitments. She does not hold on to her baggage the way she used to because she uses the releasing technique daily. Whenever anything negative comes up, she releases it and accepts the opposite, the positive.

Okay, Now What?

✴

As you identified your original commitments to your mother, father, family, family team, family spouse, ego, and family child, you saw the pattern of your life, your story. With each subsequent commitment, you got a piece of the puzzle. As you released each one, you unlocked the door to the next commitment until now you have a much clearer picture of the life you used to lead.

As you rewrote your commitments, you consciously chose your new story, and when you accepted each new commitment and its accompanying declarations, you set it into motion.

You will continue to get flashes of insight and put the pieces of your life's story together. Childhood events you may not have understood will now become clear to you. Apply these insights to what you already know, and experience the revelations as they appear.

You have completed part 1 of this book. Rest in this space for as long as you need to. You will know when the time is right to move on to Part 2. You will not need to be told. It will be perfectly clear...

PART 2

How Do You Know When You Are Ready to Move into the Magic?

✦✦

For years I have said that you do not do anything till you are good and damn ready—and that is when you will move into the Magic: when you are good and damn ready.

There is a difference between being ready and being good and *damn* ready. It is the difference between *talking* and *doing*. Here is an example:

Let's say that you want to lose weight. You think about it.

Perhaps you talk about it with your friends. You look into different diets. You even go so far as to buy a scale. (I am talking about one that actually works, not the one collecting dust in the corner of your bathroom!) You are *ready* to lose weight.

When you are good and *damn* ready to lose weight, you are out the door and on your way to join a health club.

When you are ready to move into the Magic, you know it because you cannot take your life as it is for one more minute. You have had it up to your eyeballs and you are ready for a transformation. You have one or more (or all!) of the following symptoms:

- You are ready to jump out of your skin
- You have no passion, enthusiasm or excitement for life
- You see the story of your life repeating itself over and over, even though you have done the steps in Part 1 of this book
- You see the story of your life repeating itself over and over, but you do not have the energy to stop it
- You are exhausted
- You are depressed
- You have no motivation to do anything
- You are just existing
- You feel hopeless
- You do not want to go on
- You want to do nothing but eat, sleep, read, drink, watch TV = escape
- You want sugar
- Your body hurts
- You are physically ill

- You feel hypnotized and unable to think
- You have pulled back from people
- You are frustrated, bored and fed up with your life and the people in it.

*In a nutshell, when you are ready to move into the Magic, you will know it because your life lacks **passion!***

You Gotta Have a Passion!

**

Probably the strongest indication that you are ready to move into the Magic is that your life lacks luster and passion. What once thrilled you is no longer interesting. Without a passion, life is boring. In fact, it is not a life; it is an existence.

So often our lives become humdrum. We do the same things day after day with no end or reward in sight except maybe a paycheck or a relaxing weekend. But with a passion, everything is different. We are happy, excited, and look forward to getting up in the morning.

When I told one student that she needed a passion, she said she had one: "Chocolate!" After we both laughed, I said, "That's not a passion; that's a craving!", and we laughed some more.

When I talk about a passion, I am not talking about what you feel when your favorite teams is winning, or the passion you feel when you are arguing for one of your beliefs, or even the passion you feel when you begin a new romance.

When I talk about a passion, I am talking about something that makes your heart sing when you are involved in it. Something that is so enjoyable and consuming that you lose all track of time when you are doing it. I am talking about the pure passion you feel when you are living your dream.

Finding your passion/your dream is the first step in discovering your life's mission, and discovering your life's mission moves you into the Magic.

How do you find your passion/your dream? I have found a really simple way to do this. Just ask yourself the following question: **If money were no object and success were absolutely guaranteed, what would you do for the rest of your life that would make your heart sing and thrill you down to your toes?**

Then let your heart answer the question. You might find yourself back in your childhood when you were joyfully successful at something or when you had a dream about what you wanted to be when you grew up. You knew what it was back then. All you have to do is remember it.

I recently worked with Mike, a handsome man in his late 40s. He lamented that he was out of shape, overweight, and no longer enjoyed his work. To counteract his drinking and overeating, he had bought a home exercise machine. He never used it. And he had joined a health club. He went only once. He was clearly unmotivated. Exercise alone served no purpose.

So I asked him, "Mike, if money were no object and success were absolutely guaranteed, what would you do for the rest of your life that would make your heart sing and thrill you down to your toes?"

Then I stopped talking and just listened. I knew that, in the process of talking, he would find his passion. All I had to do was listen for the clues and encourage him.

He started by saying that he would do something that would help children who lacked confidence to feel good about themselves. Then he went on to talk about his teenage years when he was made fun of and bullied. What empowered him at that time were martial arts. He told me how those classes changed him, and how good he felt about himself because he was in shape. He looked great and felt confident because he knew he could defend himself. And best of all, no one messed with him!

As he relived how he looked and felt back then, his attitude changed. He got excited = passionate! He re-experienced the joy, happiness and confidence he had felt back then, and he glowed.

Taking my cues from his story, I told him that the exercise he loved the most was martial arts. I encouraged him to sell the exercise machine, discontinue his health club membership, and invest in some martial arts classes.

His mind's first objection was that he had been away from martial arts for about thirty years, and he was overweight. (It is very common for your mind to tell you why it will not allow you to live your dream and follow your passion. All you have to do is defuse it by seeing it for what it is: an excuse.)

My response was, "So what? It will all come rushing back to you. Take it one step at a time. Remember how good you were at it and how great you felt when you were doing it." By reminding him of how good it felt, I got him out of his mind and back into his passion. (When you are doing this step and your mind shows you the excuse it has used to hold you back, simply ask yourself, "Is this the truth?" That should handle it.)

Then I told him that once he felt great about how he looked, he could share it with young people and live his dream.

He felt it. He glowed. He was back on track. His passion to set up a martial arts program for kids who lack confidence was there all along. All he had to do was get in touch with his passion for it.

Some people have always known what their passion was and simply followed their dream:

Dave, my marvelous maintenance man, had wanted to be a firefighter ever since he was a kid. His father earned his living as a maintenance man, so Dave "learned from the master" and became superb at home maintenance.

A couple of years ago, when he was almost fifty, overweight and out of shape, Dave decided to follow his passion and pursue his childhood dream of becoming a firefighter. He had to go through rigorous physical training and lose weight. He totally threw himself into it and passed all the required tests. He let nothing stand in the way of his passion.

Today, Dave is a firefighter—and on his days off, he is still a superb maintenance man.

When she was little, Julie loved to arrange the furniture in her doll house. She turned that passion into a career and became an interior designer. Then she became a realtor. When the real estate market fell, she did not let go of her passion. Instead, she kicked it up a notch and became a home stager.

Now she decorates homes that are for sale to make them attractive to potential buyers. Once the home sells, she moves the furniture to another home on the market. She has taken her childhood passion and turned it into a career.

This is how Gina described her dream/her passion:

"I would travel the world and work with other professionals to successfully plan small communities in undeveloped regions for sustainability and an improved quality of life. In the process I would make many new friends, learn about many different cultures, and complete my discovery of self. I want to open my eyes and heart, and absorb the beauty of the world by looking past my own little world. I am finding that the definition of 'family' goes far beyond the traditional, and fully embrace it. This is my measure of success."

Roberta said she would take care of her parents, daughter and grandson financially so that they never lacked for anything, or had to struggle or feel obligated to anyone for financial assistance; she would travel the world and absorb different people and cultures; she would throw a big party every couple of months and share her bounty with friends and family, and she would stop and say thanks every day for her good fortune, good life, good health, good friends and great family.

Carla said, "I would be some type of counselor. I love to help people work through their problems/ challenges and encourage them to take their next step in their growth process. I think I've been a cheerleader my whole life."

Linda said, "I would travel the world, and live and work with various cultures on a variety of matters, such as children's education, health, and whatever peaks my interest at any given point in time. I would also be involved with and a participant in some aspect of the performing arts, most likely the art form of dance."

Finding your passion is the first step in discovering your life's mission. It describes what you would *do* while you are living and expressing your mission.

So ask yourself, *If money were no object and success were absolutely guaranteed, what would I do for the rest of my life that would make my heart sing and thrill me down to my toes?*

Your heart will answer the question.

And once you know your passion, the next step is to discover your mission. This is not the time to stop and think about your passion or dream about it, this is the time to take the next and final step of discovering why you came to this planet. You are practically there. If you pause here without discovering your mission, you can easily fall back into your story, and at this point in your journey, that will feel worse than it did before because you have come so far and know so much.

So, turn the page and discover your mission.

Your Mission

✦✦

You have let go of the story that has run your life and rewritten it. You are now ready to create your new life as the powerful spiritual being that you are.

Discovering your mission is thrilling and life-transforming. It marks the end of your story and the beginning of your new life. It is a profound step because your mission is your reason for coming to planet Earth. It is the door that allows you to move into the Magic. Once you know what it is, you will resonate with it on such a deep level that there is no way you cannot express it.

Your mission has been hidden from your conscious mind, and yet, because it is so much a part of you, you have already been doing it on some level! All you have to do is bring it to consciousness and it will come alive. And this step, like all the others in this powerful book, is simple.

Just go back to your answer to the question, *If money were no object and success were absolutely guaranteed, what would you do for the rest of your life that would make your heart sing and thrill you down to your toes?* Then get out of your head and let your heart speak.

Your answer to the question is not your mission; it is your passion. It is what you would *do*. **Your mission is *why* you would do it.** So think big; think cosmically. Remember that you are talking about what your True Self came here to accomplish. Ask yourself *why* you would do your passion. And keep asking why. You will be swept along as if you were on a jet stream until, suddenly, you will get an answer that resonates so deeply within you that time stands still, when you stop breathing for a few seconds, and when you know deep in your soul that you have the answer you have searched for. This is your mission. This is why you came to planet Earth. Allow yourself to experience the indescribable feeling that comes with this realization. As you do, you will naturally move into the Magic—the Magic that is you.

As you live in the Magic, you will continue to see deeper levels of your mission. They will come to you spontaneously. When you see them, you will recognize them, and you will move into deeper levels of the Magic.

Working with a Buddy

✴✴

If you are working with a buddy and helping them discover their mission, start with the first question: *If money were no object and success were absolutely guaranteed, what would you do for the rest of your life that would make your heart sing and thrill you down to your toes?* Ask it and then let them talk. All you have to do is listen. You will notice their excitement growing as they allow their thoughts to pour out of them. Encourage them to think BIG and remind them, if necessary, that they are describing more than a job; they are describing their passion, their dream. At some point, they will tell you exactly what their passion is in their own words. This is what they want to *do* when they are living their mission.

Then ask them ask them *why* they want to do this. Watch their body language. It will change as they get closer to discovering their mission. They may start to tear up; they may shake; they may speak more quickly or more slowly. But at some point, using the words that come from their heart and resonate down to their soul, they will verbalize their mission. They will probably stop breathing for a few seconds. That will tell you they have gotten their mission. That is your signal to stop talking and allow them to move naturally into the Magic.

Peggi's Mission

✳✳

When I asked Peggi the question, *"If money were no object and success were absolutely guaranteed, what would you do for the rest of your life that would make your heart sing and thrill you down to your toes?"*, it was difficult for her to come up with anything at first. So I asked her a different question; I asked her what she loved, what her passion was.

Her two passions were nature and animals. This opened the door for her heart to express itself. She said **she would love to have a sanctuary, a retreat, where animals**

would be saved; a place where people could come to be regenerated, rejuvenated, renewed and healed. As she spoke, she burst into tears of joy. She knew she had found her passion. This is what she wants to *do* to express her mission.

Then I asked her *why* she wanted to do this. She moved into her heart and said it was because she wanted to:

- Work with abused women, children and animals
- Respect life
- Bring peace and balance to life
- Make people aware that we live in an eco-system and must live in harmony with and respect for each other, animals and nature

As she talked, she got her mission: **"To bring peace and balance to life."**

Loren's Mission

✦✦

Loren and I had worked on her mission before, and each time we worked on it, she got a deeper, larger, more powerful picture of what it was.

Loren is a natural healer/nurturer and thinks globally. She was imprisoned in the role of mother with her entire family all her life and was not allowed to nurture anyone outside the family. This severely limited her. She felt that if she could just heal her family, she would be free to move out into the world and share her gifts. She gave her family her heart, soul, mind, body, beauty, money—her life.

This time, when I asked her, *"If money were no object and success were absolutely guaranteed, what would you do for the rest of your life that would make your heart sing and thrill you down to your toes?"*, she knew what she wanted to do: she wanted to **be a doctor.** Not an MD, but, what she calls "a true doctor". This is her passion. This is what she wants to do to express her mission.

When I asked her *why* she wants to be a doctor, she said it is because **she wants to heal the planet, i.e., everyone outside her family.** This is her mission.

Marilyn's Mission

✦✦

When I asked Marilyn the question, *"If money were no object and success were absolutely guaranteed, what would you do for the rest of your life that would make your heart sing and thrill you down to your toes?"*, she said she would love to be in front of large groups of people, teaching and sharing what she is passionate about. So I asked her what that was. She said she is passionate about the *true* history of mankind, religion, science—not what we are told in the news. As we talked, she boiled her passion down to **teaching the true stories behind history.**

This is her passion and this is what she wants to *do* in the expression of her mission.

Then I asked her *why* she wants to do this. She said she believes that man has abused power and destroyed the truth. She wants to bring the truth alive so that people feel it and come out of their numbness. She wants people to arrive at the ultimate truth that they are God. By using her natural enthusiasm, inspiration, and fearless approach to people from all walks of life, **she wants to create a ripple effect that will awaken people to being open to the truth, and truly feel it and live it in this lifetime**. That is her mission.

Hope's Mission

✦✦

Hope had been thinking about her mission for some time, so when I asked her, *"If money were no object and success were absolutely guaranteed, what would you do for the rest of your life that would make your heart sing and thrill you down to your toes?"*, she had her answer: It was **to be a healer.** This is her dream, her passion. She recognizes that she is already doing this in her job as hospital Care Coordinator.

The way she does this is by helping people **face what is, deal**

with it, and find the tools to move forward. This gives them hope, and this is her mission. Her vision is to do this on a much larger scale in the nonprofit community.

What Is the Magic?

✦✦

The Magic is what you feel when you are living your mission. It is that zone you enter that is beyond definition, beyond the reach of the conscious mind. It is the space of limitless potential where creation and miracles occur. It is a place of ecstasy, joy and love.

In the Magic you are in a state of pure being. You are in the flow. You are beyond the limitations of space and time—you are in the Now of universal time. You know on a cellular level that you are one with the whole, and that you are being led, one step at a time, to exactly where you are supposed to be.

With just a thought, you can manifest what you want. All you have to do is think it, and it is on its way to you.

Access your own Magic and move into it. The Magic is in you—it IS you. Be it. Live it. And change your world.

Is This Part of
My Mission?

✳✳

Laurie had discovered her mission, accepted it and
committed to it. She was living in the Magic and
was feeling great.

As she tells it, "Shortly after I discovered my
mission and moved into the Magic, what came up
with a bang was my story.

"I'd gone out of town to visit friends, and the visit
was idyllic. We'd had such a wonderful time that

we didn't want to say good-bye.

"When I got home I got a voicemail from my daughter, Kim, who was upset about an argument she'd had with her boyfriend. The thought of sitting on the phone and listening to her complain about her life felt awful to me, yet I was torn. Kim is my daughter, and I wanted to be there for her. In the past, I would have sat on the phone with her for hours, listening to every detail of the problem, but now I knew that she was in her story and would try to pull me into it as well. So I just asked myself, 'Is this part of my mission?' The answer was a resounding 'NO!'

"Once I got my answer, I was back on purpose; I was no longer torn. We resolved the problem by emailing one another. This allowed me to be there for Kim without getting involved in a long, emotional conversation which could pull me into her story, and helped her solve the problem with her boyfriend."

Laurie's experience illustrates how the people in your life who are still in their stories will continue to try to control you so that you will take care of them by giving them what they want. You do not want to get drawn back into your story, but you may be torn. You may be very close to these people, and feel obligated to give them your attention and help them. This will take your attention off your mission if you allow it. All you have to recognize is that they are in their story and you are not, and make up your mind that nothing and no one can take your focus off your mission.

Then ask yourself, "Is this part of my mission?" The answer will give you your next move.

The bottom line is this: you are either in your story or in the Magic.

After the Magic

✦✦

Once you have discovered your mission, accept it, commit to it and act on it. And keep acting on it. Watch it expand and keep taking it to the next level as you live in the Magic. After all, your mission is your destiny and the reason you came to planet Earth in the first place.

If you do not act on it, you will find yourself caught in limbo between the Magic and your story. If this occurs, you will re-experience the symptoms you had before you discovered it, which can be painful. You can actually go back into your story, and this will be extremely painful.

Once you have experienced the ecstasy of moving into the Magic, the universe will show you what is keeping you from staying there: every false belief and everything about yourself that is untrue and holding you back. Your buttons will get punched and you will see yourself, your beliefs and your story as never before. You may even question if you have released your original commitments to them. You have. You are simply seeing how you have created and lived your story in the past. Your mind is now revealing your core blocks and limiting beliefs. This is a time of purification.

How will you see your beliefs? Through the people in your life. They will act as your mirror. Whatever you resent or dislike about them, whatever angers or upsets you about them is what you have in yourself. These traits will be magnified so you can see them clearly. They may not be pretty or feel comfortable. However, they are surfacing so you can let them go.

You have the choice of blaming and criticizing the people who are punching your buttons, or being grateful to them for being your mirror. If you blame and criticize them, you can take on the role of victim and move back into your story; if you take your responsibility for creating your own life, you will recognize them as your greatest teachers and be grateful for them.

All you have to do is identify what they are showing you, release it, and accept the opposite. Then remind yourself why you are here (your mission) and who you are (God in earthly form), and you will move back into the love, joy and bliss of the Magic.

Teresa was at a dinner party where Tom, a control

freak, was the host. He bossed his guests around and barked orders at them all evening. His need to have things perfect made everyone uncomfortable, especially Teresa. For days after the party, all she could talk about was how rude, selfish and controlling Tom was. She said she would never attend any of his parties again.

Teresa did not realize that Tom had shown her her *own* need to be in control, which is why she reacted so strongly to *his*. He was being her mirror. Once she realized this, she took her responsibility for having created the situation with Tom. She released her need to be in control. She accepted that she was free from controlling, and she accepted people just as they are. Then she reminded herself of her mission and moved back into the Magic. After doing these steps, she appreciated Tom and was grateful to him for helping her see what was keeping her from staying in the Magic.

Sometimes you will just see something in yourself that you want to release. You will know what it is because it will hit you right between the eyes.

Maggie was at the car dealership because of a recall on her car. The dealership offered to repair the problem and replace the original floor mats. In order to save money at the time she had purchased her car, Maggie had not bought the manufacturer's mats. Instead, she had gone to an auto supply store and bought some generic ones. She was excited about the possibility of finally getting a set of manufacturer's mats.

However, when the service rep noticed that she did not have the original mats in her car, he asked her if she had ever had them. She lied. She said she had had them at one time, but had replaced them with a generic brand. The rep told her that the dealer could only replace the manufacturer's mats.

The minute Maggie told her lie, she felt awful. She was horrified that she would lie, especially about something as unimportant as car mats!

As soon as she saw what she had done, without even thinking about it, she flashed back to her childhood. As a child, she had always told the truth, but her mother did not believe her. She saw her mother lie and exaggerate, and she emulated this behavior in order to be believed. She also flashed on different times in her adult life when she had told the truth, but was not believed. She saw these incidents in a split second.

She released her need to lie, accepted that she tells the truth, reminded herself of her mission, and moved back into the Magic.

She was grateful that she had not been able to fool the service rep. If she had, every time she would have looked at those mats she would have felt guilty.

If a situation arises and you are having trouble identifying what it is trying to show you, just ask yourself, "What do I have to be right about?" The answer to this question is one of your limiting core beliefs. All you have to do is release the belief, and accept the opposite, then think of your mission and move back into the Magic. The change in how you feel will be dramatic—and heavenly.

> Connie had always believed that she was unlovable and unwanted. This created an underlying sadness within her. When she realized that she was hanging on to this belief in order to defend her story and be right, she was amazed! When she let it go and moved back into the Magic she felt as if a whole new world had opened up for her.

If you have asked, "What do I have to be right about?", but are not getting a clear answer, the reason is simple: excuses. Your mind is showing you how it uses your story and the people and events in it as an excuse to keep you from living your mission, to keep you from being your most powerful, your most extraordinary, your most magical. That's all. This realization is often all you need for instant clarity. You will probably feel relieved and happy just to know the cause of the problem. Then, simply let go of excuses, accept that you let nothing stand in your way, remind yourself of your mission, and move back into the Magic.

> Don had completed a project that would launch a new career for him, and he was excited about it until his mind told him why it might not work. Then he lost his excitement and began to doubt himself and the project. However, when he realized that his mind was simply giving him an excuse for failure, he saw it clearly and his thinking was transformed. He decided that nothing, including his own mind, would stop him from living his mission. Just this one realization propelled him forward.

Shh... It's a Secret!

✸✸

When you first discover your mission, you will
feel like you are ready to levitate. Your aches
and pains will move to the back burner. You
will be so thrilled and in love with life that you will want
to tell everyone about your mission. Don't. You read that
correctly. Do not share your mission with just anyone. Why?
Because the negative people in your life will be threatened by
your joy and feel that they are losing control over you. They
are. So they will try to destroy your joy, your passion and
your mission. If you are not solid in your mission, they can

take it away from you, i.e., they can pull you down where fear and doubt can replace joy, hope and optimism. You can lose your vision, doubt yourself and be back in your story.

Several years ago I met Bob when I interviewed him to be part of a project I was working on. I went to his home to meet him because he was recovering from a serious illness. As we talked about his skills, I could see that he was charming and talented, but lacked energy and hope. His young wife was the strong one, and clearly controlled the household. I knew that if I could work with Bob for just a few minutes, I could help him find his mission, and his life would change.

So I told him about the power of discovering and living his mission—and he got excited! He was clearly ready to leap forward.

A few minutes later, his wife told us she was going to run some errands and would be back in a little while. Here was our golden opportunity.

I was able to help him find his passion and then his mission. It has been so long ago that I do not remember what they were, but I do remember his reaction. As we talked, he became more excited, animated and alive. His face glowed and his body language totally changed. His voice became stronger and his eyes became clearer. He was filled with joy and purpose. He even looked younger. He was transformed right before my eyes and moved into the Magic.

Then his wife returned. He enthusiastically shared his passion and his mission with her. Her immediate response was to remind him that he was recovering from an illness and to put his attention on that.

In an instant, everything about him changed. He lost his joy, his enthusiasm and his optimism. His face fell, his sadness returned, and he looked like a tired old man. He was back in his story and out of the Magic. With one sentence, his wife had destroyed his hope and taken back control of his life. There was nothing more I could do.

From time to time I think about him and wonder how his recovery went. I hope he saved his notes from our session—and I hope he rediscovered his mission and moved back into the Magic.

Borrow the Magic

✦✦

If you are faced with a situation so upsetting that you come out of the Magic, a simple way to move back into it is to borrow the Magic from an earlier event in your life. Think of some wonderful event you experienced, perhaps when you were a child, that transformed your life and changed you. Move into the feeling of that event and apply it to your current situation. The results are powerful.

> Growing up, Carol's mother compared her to other children and commented on their beauty.

Carol never measured up. As a result, she never felt she was pretty.

When she was in college, her sorority entered her in the largest beauty pageant on campus. That surprised her! However, you can imagine her shock when she was selected as one of the ten finalists! Her first thought was, "My mother lied to me all these years!" From that moment on, her life totally changed. She gained a self-confidence she had never had. She felt beautiful and saw the world differently.

Now, whenever Carol wants to borrow the Magic, all she has to do is remember this turning point in her life, and she is there. She stays in the feeling of being a beauty pageant finalist, applies it to her current situation, and stays in the Magic.

Living in the Magic

✴✴

Ronnie and her husband lived in a beautiful townhome community that had recently converted to condominiums. The units were very popular and they all sold. Ronnie and her husband had two months in which to find a new home and move. They found a brand new community that was under construction and bought their dream house. The builder told them that their home would be ready in two months. While this was cutting it close to the deadline, Ronnie knew they could do it.

Unfortunately, the weather did not cooperate. Rain, snow and ice halted construction for awhile and prevented the sheetrock from drying. Their builder then told them that their home would not be ready on the date promised. This meant they would have to put their furniture in storage and move themselves and their two cats into a motel or her in-laws' home for awhile. Neither of these alternatives was acceptable to Ronnie.

Ronnie is a student of Truth. She knew that she and her husband had created this problem and that they could change it and consciously create it the way they wanted. Plan A was to move into their home on the original date. There was no Plan B.

The negativity from their builder's daily phone calls was too upsetting for Ronnie, so her husband responded to them. This allowed Ronnie to stay positive.

She reminded herself that she is infinite, immortal Spirit in an earthbound body, felt the joy of living her mission (to empower people), moved into the blissful feeling of the Magic and applied it to the completion of their home and their move into it. In essence, she borrowed the Magic. She visualized and lived in the happiness of living in their new home all day every day.

Once the builder realized that Ronnie and her husband were serious about moving in on the original date, he shifted into high gear. He brought space heaters into the house to dry the sheetrock and did everything necessary to complete the construction on time.

On the day they had originally planned, Ronnie, her husband, and their two cats moved into their new home. The moving vans pulled into the driveway as the builder's cleaning crew was finishing up.

To this day, their builder takes credit for their miraculous move. Ronnie just smiles and lets him.

You Are...

Y ou are infinite, immortal, majestic, powerful, awesome, gloriously beautiful, radiantly healthy, abundantly wealthy Spirit in physical form. You are God in an earthbound body. This is the truth. Anything else is a lie.

You have come here with a thrilling mission. When you discover and express your mission, you move into the Magic—the Magic that is *you*.

Maxine is available for personal astrological readings, healing sessions and spiritual coaching sessions. For information on her services, please visit her websites: www.maxinetaylor.com or www.moveintothemagic.com. If you would like information on when and where Maxine will be presenting her Move Into the Magic Workshop, and if you would also like to receive her free monthly newsletter, simply visit her websites and ask to be placed on her mailing list.

CPSIA information can be obtained
at www.ICGtesting.com
Printed in the USA
BVHW032244310520
580474BV00002B/323